A UNITED STATES CITIZEN OPINION

A UNITED STATES CITIZEN OPINION

FRAN WALKER

A United States Citizen Opinion
Copyright © 2020 by Fran Walker. All rights reserved.

No part of this publication may be reproduced, stored in a retrieval system or transmitted in any way by any means, electronic, mechanical, photocopy, recording or otherwise without the prior permission of the author except as provided by USA copyright law.

The opinions expressed by the author are not necessarily those of URLink Print and Media.

1603 Capitol Ave., Suite 310 Cheyenne, Wyoming USA 82001
1-888-980-6523 | admin@urlinkpublishing.com

URLink Print and Media is committed to excellence in the publishing industry.

Book design copyright © 2020 by URLink Print and Media. All rights reserved.

Published in the United States of America
ISBN 978-1-64753-540-7 (Paperback)
ISBN 978-1-64753-541-4 (Digital)

21.10.20

Acknowledgment

…Because God created the earth and is the creator of ALL mankind.

I give thanks to my Creator for shadowing me through my experiences in life. My journey has given me the courage to write this book. I thank him for providing me with wisdom to share my personal view as a citizen of the United States. Through my trials and tribulations, I give praise and thanks for life endurance and joy.

I started writing this book a few years ago. I would like to acknowledge two great kings, my son Michael R. Payne and youngest son Eszavion L. Franklin, Jr. They have been my blessing reasons for continuing in life with the upmost praises to God! To be a proud mother of two amazing creatures that exists today. I love you both unconditionally for life!

I thank my cousin Charles Walker for support. My cousin Garry, Stacey, for their conversations of hope and faith. My brother friends in Christ, Frederick, Eugene, and others for acknowledging me as a Godly Woman of God. For uplifting me in prayers and believing in my gifts, Checha Reddy and Miriam Miller. Jane, Lorna, Denise, Rogerlin and others, thanks for positive "girl talk" motivation. I give honor and thanks to God for my deceased parents, siblings, many nieces and nephews, family, and friends. A special individual thanks to everyone for all your support and prayers!

If you live long enough, you would have seen it all.
Why…
Because life is a cycle…we repeat what others have done or we break an old traditional cycle and begin another broken cycle…

I am sure that I am not the only one who is willing to voice an opinion on living as a citizen in the United States and not get ridiculed for doing so. I remain babble with the attempts made by man to rebuild an existing foundation which mankind has no bearing on. I was compelled to write this book based on my opinion and overall experience living as a United States citizen.

Although, the United States still has many benefits, are they worth the claim as a citizen? To what extreme does one claim a right of citizenship? The foundation is cracking within sight, and the "law engineers" are all embedded in history. The embedded ones have left a blue print that hinders mankind to build on the Creator's soil.

I was born into this unrealistic government system that works on a temporary fix. Struggling as a citizen to survive in an economy controlled with limited plans to work in the future. The sole purpose of the dirt from the ground was to build, but it destroys its very purpose to life. As I continue to plow my indefinite life in this country on a soil of cracking foundation, an American dream is falling right before my eyes! As I age with time, the dream slowly travels behind me. Live long enough and you will begin to "live by faith and not by sight."

Through my years, I have seen presidents of the United States of America voted in and out of their office terms. I begin to notice a change as a citizen with the Bushes, which I was concern with my rights as a citizen living in the United States. Now that we have President Obama, I am saddened that more uncertainty is to come as he remains in office, and unknown disasters to come when his term ends. Our president's leadership has been continuously blocked by opposing forces.

A United States Citizen Opinion

The American Citizens Helpmate, with all due respect to Michelle Obama has become one of the key sources to placing this country on track to a solid spiritual nation, which would become an honor to live in as a citizen. Our president reminds me of a painting I once saw on the wall of a Salisbury City government office in North Carolina. It caught my eyes while I waited to address some business matters. It read as follows:

"Leadership"
The speed of the ladder determines the rate of the pack.

President Obama is not an idol, but he seems to be one of the anointed helpers to possibly lead this country under God. In a public speech in 1799, Patrick Henry quoted, "United we stand, divided we fall." He was a politician who led the movement for independence in Virginia 1770s. He opposed the United States Constitution, fearing that it endangered the rights of the states, as well as the freedom of individuals. The American dream is said to be a national ethos or custom of the United States in which freedom includes a promise of the possibility of prosperity and success. James Traslow Adams, in 1931, defined the American dream: "Life should be better and richer and fuller for everyone, with the opportunity for each according to ability and achievement regardless of social class or circumstances of birth."

Declaration of Independence proclaims that "all men are created equal," and that they are "endowed by their Creator with certain unalienable rights including, Life, Liberty and the pursuit of happiness." Will Smith, a gifted and talented actor, portrayed natural law in the movie *The Pursuit of Happyness*. Gardner was faced with all kinds of adversity, one after the other, and finally he falls flat on his back. The story picks up showing the trials and tribulation to get back on track.

"Rejoicing in hope; patient in tribulation; continuing instant in prayer" (Rom. 12:12, KJV). "My brethren, count it all joy when ye fall into divers temptations" (James 1:2, KJV). The government and the media try to keep politics and religion separate, yet our government creed is based upon religion. What a mess of confusion and contradiction. If we are to have a united country, then we must all form under the same leadership, one God! "Do not be called leaders; for one is your Leader, that is, Christ" (Matt. 23:10, NASB). Of course the embedded ones had no idea that this country would begin to fall in division due to lack of God in leadership.

We need to revise the president term and vote Obama to remain in office as president indefinite as other political offices has embedded their terms. We need a president like Obama to remain in office, unless he is proven to be mentally incompetent to perform his presidential duties. If there was a question to his ability to perform, I am sure we can assume that Michelle would be the first to show signs if he were to become unfit to fulfill his duties. Since he has been in office, as a citizen I have been more informed as to the role of our president. He utilizes the media to talk to the people on changes that needs to take place because this country, as well as the people, is changing. President Obama have walked the streets and talked with people who live and have fought on them. He has visited homes of so many and has even taken time to fellowship with citizens of this country of all mankind. Our president reaches out in such natural formalities that people of all parts of the world are drawn to his distinctive personality.

Unfortunately, the roots of the "embedded ones" continue to rally against him, blocking the changes that our country is long overdue on its course. I believe citizens of this country should decide on the changes to revise the terms that a president serves and make it effective with President Obama. Why do the citizens of this country allow the embedded ones outside of the biblical ancestors of Abraham tribe to degrade our president? This despicable fouling has leaped into other countries that seem to join in on the degrading of our leadership. President Obama's overall presentation is excellent. Michelle's smile shows he has love in his heart. He has been blessed with awesome communication skills. His immediate family shows that he's very supportive. Mr. Barack is brilliant with all his effective speeches. (My observation is that he's one of the few who can clearly speak.) He is well-spoken, he has a diverse personality, highly educated, and as my niece would say, "Fine!" Finally someone with exceptional characteristics has been elected with the capability to help rebuild America's foundation under one God, and he is ridiculed and abused by the roots of the embedded ones.

We have allowed political leaders and nonacting Christians to remain in office that lack presentation, untrained verbal skills, and far from integrity. A high percentage of this country's decision makers are millionaires. These members get fat rich and neglect our needs as citizens. Some has become so disrespectful, and they fight for personal gain. "If there is a poor man among your brothers in any of the towns of the land that the LORD your God is giving you, do not be hardhearted or tightfisted toward your poor brother" (Deut. 15:7, NIV). We have created major problems by allowing Speaker John Boehner to remain in the seat. I would like to have the honor on behalf of the United

States citizens' to ask for the speaker's resignation ASAP! He applies his personal views over the rights of the citizens.

The constitution's first three words are: "We the People." Framers (embedded ones) drafted the constitution to control or oversee our society, which created a political system. The ultimate source of power rests with the people, who are the popular sovereignty. We live in this country as citizens, but society continues to remain secretly embedded by the framers who planted the Articles of Confederation. This wickedness prevents our nation from any necessary change. This is why we the people must take a stand and demand reformation for the sake of the American future!

The news today is unpleasant to watch. The wealthy voices are controlling the media and satirizing our president. Citizens must understand the speaker is supposed to be a respectable, decent individual who believe in what this country should stand for, God. Our speaker doesn't show any care to what's right and what's best for the people. He opposes our leader, and we should relieve him of his duties immediately. The speaker has been in battle with Obama prior to election and has remained embedded with his forefathers. I am ashamed that he is a voice that the world has heard on behalf of the United States.

"And the tongue is a fire, a world of iniquity: so is the tongue among our members, that it defiles the whole body, and setteth on fire the course of nature; and it is set on fire of hell" (James 3:6, KJV).

Of course, when you check ownership and control, wealth has allowed individuals to come on the air in full force by any means necessary to sanction our president's leadership abilities. These representatives fight with manipulation and injustice.

President Obama is human just like the inconsiderate people who try to make him out to be a beast of their kind. As a citizen, this seems to be the norm on how the United States is doing business. Well, the time has come for this country to change for the good or continue down the road of destruction toward another fallen country. The media should try knocking on doors of the American citizens and ask the people how they feel about our country. There is no need to ask me because I have chosen to go public with my book and put my opinions in black and white.

I love this country and its entire people. It's just that the United States have lost its basic principles of respect! I have an old saying: "Give me respect, and I can run for life." This country is a big entertainment network. There is always something to do in any area of excitement within America. "Thank God for America!" You can enjoy yourself solo, in pairs, or a group.

Entertainment in this country comes with a big price to pay. It seems the rich can pay the ticket and those less fortunate have to sacrifice a need to be a part of the entertainment. Although we claim to have some recession, we somehow have preserved the funds to smile. United States is a free country that advertises that the sky is the limit! Well, limited to those who can afford to fly in it. The wealthy gets richer, and the less fortunate get poorer. How can a poor citizen reach a goal when they can not afford the flight, left alone reach the sky?

For the kingdom of heaven of heaven is like a landowner who went out early in the morning to hire workers for his vineyard. And after agreeing with the workers for the standard wage, he sent them into his vineyard. When it was about nine o'clock in the morning, he went out again and saw others standing around in the market place without work. And he said to them, "You go into the vineyard too and I will give you whatever is right." So they went. When he went out again about noon and three o'clock that afternoon, he did the same thing. And about five o'clock that afternoon he went out and found others standing around, and he said to them, "Why are you standing here all day without work?" They said to him, "Because no one has hired us." He said to them, "You go and work in the vineyard too." When it was evening, the owner of the vineyard said to his manager, "Call the workers and give the pay starting with the last hired until the first." When those hired about five o'clock came, each received a full day's pay. And when those hired first came, they though they would receive more. But each one also received the standard wage. When they received it, they began to complain against the landowner, saying, "These last fellows worked one hour, and you have made them equal to us who bore the hardship and burning heat of the day. And the landowner replied to one of them, "Friend, I am not treating you unfairly. Didn't you agree with me to work for the standard wage? Take what is yours and go. I want to give this last man the same as I gave to you. Am I not permitted to do what I want with what belongs to me? Or are you envious because I am generous? So the last will be first, and the first will be last." (Matt. 20:1–16, ESV)

Now I do believe that there are a percentage of people who do not put an effort to stretch towards the sky. If a citizen had no past relationship with the embedded fathers of this country, they never had a chance to reach the opportunities that this country claims to be in the sky. Granted, there are some citizens who have worked successfully to get a piece of the sky. Of course, we have those who step over other citizens to grasp for the sky and are reaping from the crop that belongs to others. What about partial citizens or nicknamed citizens or aka immigrants. They have no connections to the embedded fathers or citizens but yet given the opportunities to reach the limits in the sky!

I am for all mankind and equal treatment for all. Does this country owe an unknown debt that has resulted to immigration? Legal and illegal immigrants open up businesses and become political leaders within communities. I understand that some Americans do not produce the best work and dependability. However, if every person is treated equally the same, regardless of their status, then there would be no immigration. The United States citizenship needs to be removed, because the benefits are greater as a noncitizen. I am asked to show proof of citizenship for the basic citizen benefits. This is because I am not considered a threat or an asset to this country. A criminal must show proof because they force change, which is a threat to America. All other noncitizens automatically reap the benefits as a citizen of this country.

I understand that the United States have a matter at stake with immigration. Over the past five to ten years, I noticed an overgrowth of immigration. In some states, they have overly populated the residencies. They have taken the jobs that once were given to nonskilled citizens. You eat from their hands in which food is being prepared in restaurants today. Immigrants are living in communities among taxpayers. Noncitizens are over flooding the school classrooms by executing the No Child Left Behind Policy. They are draining the limited government assistance programs for the poor and needy. The medical providers are struggling to maintain care to authorized medical beneficiaries. The borders are not maintained, and our government continues to justify poor excuses for prevention of immigration. People should not be forced to compete against one another for life in this country.

However, this country needs to get a grip on the census and capacity. The ticket counter must close once it meets the capacity of the ship. If it exceeds the maximum load allowed, it could possibly sink without warning due to an overload of passengers. Our body is the same; if we exceed the mass body weight that our flesh can handle, the health problems begin. The poor people can not afford to help immigration, so who are allowing them to enter? Precisely, my point. Everyone should have a right to live anywhere on this earth, but is it the same after death? Are evil people and godly people sharing the same destiny after death?

It says in John 3:3 (ESV), "Jesus answered him, 'Truly, truly, I say to you, unless one is born again he cannot see the kingdom of God.'" You must apply for heaven with stake in Jesus, and there must be a capacity because everyone is not going to make it in. Why do people feel the need to tear down this country? Let us work together to get control of and change the system. ~~then~~ Through this, all people can enter into this country and automatically become citizens. This world is not my home; I am just a body traveling through! Depending on what part of the United States you are from, there is a language barrier of communication. However, if you speak little or no English, there is a possibility of absolutely no communication! Unfortunately, this country encourages other languages, which contribute to the barriers in communication among all people. You can visit America anytime and decide you wanted to remain, and the red carpet gets roll out right away! No one goes to your previous countries to investigate in person your whereabouts, proof of your ID (we give you one), no visitation is made to validate your previous address, background check is limited, so your past history, credit, education, medical history, criminal background becomes obsolete. Immigration political leaders have granted citizenship with excellent credit, eligible for education, and government assistance. United States government simply makes you comfortable and gives you a key to the country. Let's not forget a blank check to write any amount you need to meet your financial needs, and no time to repay! The government puts more trust in noncitizens than natural citizenship.

The action of our government system brings about division and dysfunction in our country. A lot of factors contribute to family division and dysfunction in the United States. Generation after generation of families has been repeating the same cycle with failed results. The government is so far out of this country assisting with rebuilding lives and structures and defense but offers useless financial help toward helping structure the American families. The same resources used to help aid other countries needs to be steered towards this country. When you cannot find work to provide for your family/dependents, most people take the least responsible way and walk away from their responsibilities within a family.

Depending on your nationality or upbringing, some walk into another relationship and start another family under the same principles, none. There are families that had not yet recouped from historical embeddedness from previous controlling framers. Other families are cursed from their hereditary dysfunctional families. The upside-down crashing of the financial market crisis has sent many families into a storm. The storms keep raging and raging in my life, and it has taken away all assets or credit they had reserved towards building a bright future. Stress comes with having a family, because now you must incorporate your needs, your significant other's needs, and children's needs, while addressing your wants, your significant other's wants, your children's wants, and maintain your health, your significant other's health, your children's health, and so on... Stress leads to mental issues, now you must consider your mental capacity, your significant other's mental stage, and wonder about what are your children's mental thoughts are. With or without a job, the housing market theft has left many Americans wondering where they will lay their head to rest.

The Bible says, "The thief comes only to steal and kill and destroy; I came that they may have life, and have it abundantly" (John 10:10). Until you become victimized in this homeless arena, you have no clue what it is like to have a housing crisis. Families have fallen below bankruptcy. What financial institution or friend will grant a loan to assist in the reestablishing of your life when you have a below credit rating? These family issues are resulting from our unrealistic government system. While the Congress and political representatives continue fighting among themselves and ridiculing our president's character, we the citizens of the United States struggle to provide for our families. There needs to be guidelines and financial assistance to help strengthen American families so that we may harvest into the future of this country.

Unfortunately, there are families headed by feminist individuals, which lacks masculine structural support. Obviously this country is confused with relationship. However, it takes men, women, pet, teachers, doctors, accountants, lawyers, law enforcers, firemen, cooks, farmers, engineers, all of mankind, a village, and the fear of God to have a functional family! Family requires support, and you can not have a family if you are unable to maintain or get a job to support them.

A few years ago, the government did issue a three-hundred-dollar stimulus check to citizens. Compared to bailing out the financial money eaters, the citizens did receive funds for a month worth of bread. "For the love of money is a root of all kinds of evil. Some people, eager for money, have wandered from the faith and pierced themselves with many griefs" (1 Tim. 6:10). Jobs today require special degrees, additionally on-the-job experiences. How can one gain experiences before the job? Umm. United States government, with the private sector, employs workers from other countries and immigrants with no reference to the labor law. The government jobs require a scholar to complete the application process, and it helps to be an immigrant who has been given perfect credit.

One of our government organizations that are a prime example of unfair employment practices is the Veteran Affairs. The illegal buddy practice, or "clicks", or "friends and family tag a job" is way out of control. Management seems to be on some sort of coding operation method. You can walk into the work area and see the overload of work and the need to hire more workers. Yet, our selfish government system has the embedded forefathers' ways, preventing citizens from working. People in positions have no education, no prior work experiences, no management skills, no verbal or written communication skills, and absolutely no concern for the care of veterans. How can a nonmilitary person oversee a veteran-care operation? This is why the system is foul and continues to crack in all areas.

I have met and worked with individuals who have no right to be an employee of this organization. However, I've also known of others who *should* be employed under this organization. They can really make a difference in the care for the veterans. Trillions of dollars are given away to countries that caused veterans' lives and handicapped and wounded some. How can the United States be so quick to giveaway funds that can strengthen family lives in this country? I am a veteran, and I, too, fight for care and is given no financial assistance to reestablish my life and family.

The media is on this kick about mental health. How much do you think a person can take as they watch the financial help given to other countries, which have no impact on the citizens' lives of this country? Our country has priority in rebuilding other countries that less than 1 percent of United States citizens will never visit. Americans cannot speak their language, and these countries despise Americans. Why are trillions of dollars given away to noncitizens? This is why I say you can benefit more as a noncitizen.

I have a suggestion: give another stimulus check in the amount of twenty-five to fifty thousand dollars. This suggested amount will stimulate the economy in cross ways. The money-saving citizens would deposit their funds into the banks. Some citizens will make foolish choices, and the robbers and thieves will gain. A percentage of people will upgrade rental or put down on a financing a home. Some will remodel their homes, and then construction workers and real estate industry will grow. The furniture and shopping stores will boom in sales. The auto industry will grow in production of vehicles. Some citizens would travel or vacation. The loan servicers will profit from citizens who want to invest and use their credit. Creditors will get paid, moving more people out of the bankruptcy courts, which will allow the courts to breathe from over loaded of cases. The education system will survive from unpaid student loans. This stimulus check will boost the economy.

The private sector, however, has selfishly placed a freeze on hiring because the government has allowed them to do whatever they want. To get a job that pays enough to live as an average-income citizen, you have to be in shape, have ran a marathon, have relation with upper management, no children to call off from work, two master's degrees (in case one is not accepted), never visited the court house, speak no English, open to any shift, and a noncitizen. When you apply for a job, you have to compete with thousands of other applicants for that one generated position. Most Americans are no longer motivated to seek work because the system is not motivated to hire.

Some representatives within all forms of our government system should be ashamed for lack of humanity and resign from his or her position. The United States has pledged on one nation under God. Why do we allow any and every religious practice presented by man on earth to come and worship their idol gods? Perhaps we need clarity as to what God does this country worship and honor? Maybe, to claim citizenship, it would help if this pledge was defined. Is the United States that weak in standing firm in what it believes in? Is God, the Father, Jesus the Son, and the Holy Spirit, which we pledge? This country has become confused and has allowed any and individual (to include noncitizens) to impose their religious beliefs in this country? Individual(s) can visit the USA and build a temple(s) symbolizing and honoring their unknown god. Our government system continues to pledge to the embedded rules to govern this country and now the immigration (candidates and leaders) has studied these rules and busting open the leaks within this country government rules.

Immigration has become a way to beat this country at its own game. Obviously, the original plan was to use immigrants for labor and other personal use. However, immigrants now are becoming educated, strong in numbers, and wealthy political leaders. Our school system is a big joke. If the children are our future, then why are we having such a hard time investing in them? The teachers are with our children as parents, and the parents should become co-parents to these educators. Most schools are in dying needs of upgrading structures and new technologies to prepare for the future. Violence has leaped into our schools placing distraction on academic study. For this matter, the government should consider increasing security, upgrading entry, and providing monitor services. This upgrade in security will keep discipline and safety under control. United States invests into foreigners to attend American schools for free, and they pick up their masters and return back home leaving their taxes unpaid. The teachers deserve to have higher pay. We pay congress, and they invest nothing into us or our future.

The government system is blind and is in deep need of new, changing minds. Invest in our future, and watch these young brilliant minds flow out from the citizens. The mind is a terrible thing to waste. It is so important to work with the generation gap to have effective communication for all. "Finally, be ye all of one mind, having compassion one for another. Love each other as brethren, be sympathetic, be courteous" (1 Pet. 3:8). America must understand that every citizen plays an important role to this country's stability. We, as people, must learn to live together out of respect. Granted, everyone has chosen their own lifestyle to live. However, there is a grey area that we all must avoid to allow others to live. So, we must not continue to take on this attitude, saying this is the way I am or am grown, for this ignorance keeps us fallen in the grey area affecting others, especially ourselves. Then we must not continue to assume the tradition. I am not going to change, when right before our eyes the country is changing. All mankind must assume the attitude that it is not about me, but about change for the future.

The image of our children in the United States is ungrateful and selfish, just like this country's founding fathers. Although debatable since this social issue is indeed rampant, I suggest usage of simpler sentences since there is no report cited within the manuscript. | Children nowadays no longer hold respect for others, or even themselves. They are lost traveling on different pathways leading nowhere. Are families raising enemies in their homes? Are we strangers living among our children? We must have hope for the children in this country. Some parents are not financially able or mature enough to handle raising children. Most parents are still dealing with their own unpractical childhood experience. A percentage of parents are successful in raising a child, and their success is passed on.

The money that our government and the wealthy citizens donate to other countries should be invested in the children who are citizens of your American home. There is always a list published to show the wealthiest people. I would like to see the list of poor people. Children are homeless here in the United States, and they attend our government schools. I would like to see the list of people whom the government claims they're helping and ask them if their life above poverty? Who are the politicians helping, certain not the children of this countries future. Let us try to strengthen our children because they are the ones that will care for you when you can no longer help yourself. This country is lost with the future outlook of American youth. It is unrealistic to believe or trust the leaders of the United States. Our children no longer believe in us as parents for guidance. The people no longer have faith in this historical government system. American people need to humble as a whole and seek the

Almighty God. Causing physical trauma onto someone, killing, fighting, domestic violence, rape, violating others, riots, robbing/stealing, cheating, kidnapping, scandalizing and defaming one's character, manipulating, adultery, cheating, traumatizing, terrorizing, falsification, gang banging, disrespecting, cursing, murder, sexual abuse, negative attitudes, hatred, and all other inexcusable actions need to cease.

"But the things that proceed out of the mouth come from the heart, and those defile the man" (Matt. 15:18). Instead of expanding and building prisons and jails, upgrade existing ones with high technologies. Vote in place a No Tolerance policy for inexcusable actions. Exercise one offense and eliminate the options for repeated offenses and citizens will avoid making these consequences and become accountable for their own actions. If you make a place comfortable, no one leaves, and people will return as many times allowed. However if the cells are just walls, overcrowded, same meals served daily, no enjoyment, a person will think twice before making a foolish, selfish, ungodly action.

The Obama's administration and the Congress got caught up in politics among themselves that little change has been done to benefit the people. Leave President Obama alone so that he may improve the change that is so needed and support the reformation of our government system. Yes we can if the blockers move to the football field and out of politics. Please get off the president with all that media nonsense and allow him to complete his duties. There are too many guidelines and policies on rights for inmates. This is another system that needs to be simplified. The government should make jail time with no benefits and no privileges. Incarcerated individuals should be given no further education. The rehabilitation should be towards counseling and better communication to live in society with other people. Have these individuals help assist with cleaning and rebuilding our country. If war should break out, send most of them since they have the mind of no care as to others.

Unfortunately, the American dream of home ownership has drastically fallen off the goal list. The government leaders did not get forced out of their homes, and so there is no compassion for the citizens' foreclosure homes. In fact, they have maintained and improved their existing homes. Most homeowners live in outdated properties today due to lack of income and bad credit. It's sad when the government knows the citizens are homeless, yet they take away the rights to become a homeowner in this country. President Obama has nothing to do with this injustice of our government. The takers and most makers of the law are the ones who have contributed to this bankrupt economy. The government needs to return the land once again back to the people. Regardless of the poor unrealistic conniving formula that the mortgage loan industry and third parties used, it was illegal to foreclose on properties belonging to the citizens of this country. There is probably more bank/government-owned properties and homes than there are homeless people. Shame on our unfair, manipulated, anti-citizen government system.

United States has been declining in its overall living. Prior to President Obama, the same laws and practices have been repeatedly used. The time has come that we the American citizens must stand for change. We can no longer accept a failed government system. I suggest we expand Obama's term to death like congressmen's terms and support him in making a new system that is for the citizens. For Christ's sake! He only had twelve disciples. Why do we pay so many politicians to make decisions when they have never all agreed on nothing. There is a gap between political leaders and the people. Terminate

Congress and use the billions given towards their funds and no-cost benefits to reform United States of America. Invest in the country and not the selective few. Place a freeze on immigration so that we can get a count on who is who. Terrorist stops at home. Abolish all the government programs that do not benefit the people. Stop going over water to disturb other countries. How can we mediate other countries and this country states are in the battle field of politics?

"Do not be conformed to this world, but continuously be transformed by the renewing of your minds so that you may be able to determine what God's will is—what is proper, pleasing, and perfect" (Rom. 12:2). This country is in need of restructuring and building of a solid foundation that works for the people. Take care of the citizens who help protect, and make this country strong. Help establish strength and love among families. Work on making United States a united country for which it stands for!

Have you ever gone into a government service building seeking financial help? Try going into the Social Services (Welfare) Department and apply for Medicaid, food stamps, or child care. If you are a noncitizen, no problem you will receive maximum benefits, plus. It doesn't matter if five to ten people already receive the same services under one roof. However, if you are a citizen, you will be treated like an undercover criminal with background check, will be stripped down of the little pride you had left from your circumstances, disrespected, and disapproved for inhumane reasons. However, if you should get approved, it's for the minimum or $19.47. All case workers are overly swamped with work that requires more than one person to complete. Always remember if you're not a congressman, you must work for a living.

Most government agencies disrespect people seeking help because they take it personal that this person appears physically able to pull themselves out of their problem. I have never seen or heard of anyone pulling themselves out of a hole. Government representatives act as though the funds allowed to help the people belongs to them. Until you have been in the need of basic living essentials, you have never experience self worthlessness. The people working in these positions need to be individuals who have experienced needing help. Homelessness is not the result of choice. Circumstances and lack of resources results to homelessness. Society has been based on creditability, and if you have lost all your assets and owe what you can not afford, you become stripped, and the results become the streets. The streets flash before you, you avoid them by living here and there, living with her, him, them, they, whomever, in and out shelters until you run out of rest places. You and your children cut loose in the wilderness, wondering from day to day, seeking for hope in all the wrong places. Tired of seeing death while searching for hope, you start hustling for a breakthrough. Then you realize this homelessness is a much greater problem than you can handle. One day you fall on your knees, crying and praying out for the mercy of God to rescue you from homelessness. Finally, you receive a breakthrough, and you're being pulled out of the hole. There is no need for us to continue being grabs in a bucket—no one escapes—it's either all or none.

I find it difficult to talk about health care. If you're not the medical providers, you're the researchers for health care. If you're not the pharmacists, you're the technicians. If your not the CDC workers, then you're the law makers. And if you're not the Creator, then you're the patient. This is why there is confusion; too much input and consideration is involved to better health care. If everyone was considered the same as human, then care would be offered to anyone anytime. The money has been allocated for Congress, their family, their best friends, and their pets. Let us not that mention for pennies, the average worker pays for this to happen. Why do we continue to battle over who should get care when we are suppose to all fall under humanity. How in this country one sleep when there are people in need of medical care and in some cases life threats. How sad. With all the sources of financial capital available that we give away to help aid other countries, every citizen of the United States should have access to *free* medical care. People living arrangements, unhealthy diets, little income or lack thereof all triggers additional health matters. Old age in this country need to receive better options of care. Medical information and billing are not updated and accessible for staff and patients. Noncitizens are allowed to utilize medical care with no out-of-pocket contribution. The cost to have medical health care is outrageous.

Is it possible that this country's population is an indefinite count times the census? In other words, does United States have any idea who is in this country? Why are we discussing abortion? Why are we supporting an ungodly decision or an immature decision that efforts or impact one's future? What is the maturity level of my thoughts when making a rational decision on life or death? Do I have that right spiritually? Like most things in life, if there is no guide, we react to the situation. The decisions we make actually reflect the desires of our heart. My choice to abort may be due to my season in life. "To every thing there is a season, and a time to every purpose under the heaven: A time to be born, and a time to die; a time to plant, and a time to plunk up that which is planted; A time to kill, and a time to heal; a time to break down, and a time to build up" (Ecc. 3:1–3, KJV). Women are having babies, but the fathers are far out of sight, and in some cases, unacceptable to the birth. If this cycle is broken, then there will be less immigration and fewer women in the hospitals having babies with no health care or care. Accountability to one's choices and sexual decisions needs to be explored to help make better choices.

Health education should be another priority in this country. Although we say it is the results of this country show different. Hold the people responsible for maintaining a health diet. We assume everyone lived on the farm and was taught by big mamma how to prepare and cook a healthy meal. Big mammas are far microwave grandmas today, with exception of a few like myself. The law should mandate consumers that their mass body weight must be in range. The skin can only hold but so much body fat! Every citizen should have access to an exercise fitness gym. Tax the fast food industry and fine the media; then they would get a grip on what they are serving and advertising to the people. Americans need not concern themselves much with food poisoning, because we are slowly killing ourselves by eating unhealthy.

Another suggestion would be to terminate Congress and other political leaders' contract. Why should we the people take care of members who do not provide for our needs. This is absurd.

Child support is a book by itself. If I had to choose a topic besides a United States citizen's opinions, it would be American child support. Child support is so broad because it covers birth, care, medical, finance, housing, visitation, education, and the parent(s), just a few mentioned. In family law and public policy, child support or child maintenance is an ongoing, periodic payment made by a parent for the financial benefit of a child, following the end of a marriage or other relationship. Child maintenance is paid directly or indirectly by an obligator to an obligee for the care and support of children of a relationship that has been terminated, or in some cases never existed. Often the obligator is a noncustodial parent, a caregiver, a guardian, or the state. Child support should never be withheld as a means to punish or get revenge against the other parent.

In the same manner, access to children should never be denied because of a failure to pay child support. Financial parenting and emotional parenting are two separate matters. Children need the active presence of both parents in their lives. The Bible says children are a gift from God (Psalm 127: 3–5). When someone gives you a gift, you look after it and cherish it. Children, like gifts, need to be cherished and cared for. Now the problem with the system is that it sounds logical, but it does not produce financial support needed to provide care for the child. You mean this country system is so self-centered that it cannot establish a program that works that works to locate the absent parent? In some cases, the absentee parent is also the absent parent in other cases. When does the enforcement plug get pulled? You have mothers unwilling to provide data information to activate the child support. The sad part of this system is that the noncustodial parent goes on enjoying life without paying support. The child support system is dysfunctional. Lack of child support should become a criminal offense based on child neglect and financial abandonment. It should be taken seriously and enforced when there is no support for the child. The abandonment of children should easily be tracked through numerous sources. Shame on our government and the workers responsible for following through on the work.

The safety of the people in this country is at jeopardy more today than ever. We have no account as to who lives here or visits that are overextended. I suppose not, because we have an uncontrolled problem in knowing who is legal. We have a history of giving financial support to countries with an unrealistic payment plan and knowing that they have no intentions in doing so, ever. We interfere with other countries, and yet our system is in need of restructure. War is a cripple game, and the outcome is devastating. Lives are lost and families are ripped apart. Our country's debt and asset value has become weaken. Thanks to our President Obama for attempting to refrain from sending our troops in to fight other country's historical wars. There is a much greater war on the United States soil, and it is among the people of this country. Our government needs to consider rewriting the secretary of state's job description of foreign affairs to focus on peace among the people of the state's affairs. What is peace? Can you buy a peace of mind? Is peace a reward given for enduring long suffering? Have you seen peace being practice among people? Where is peace? Does peace comes after death? "Peace I leave with you; my peace I give to you. Not as the world gives do I give to you. Let not your hearts be troubled, neither let them be afraid" (John 14:27).

Veterans are among the worst treated citizens alongside with the poor. We sacrifice our time to protect, and some unfortunate life is given, and the gratitude from Congress is unjustifiable. Veterans deserve to be better taken care of, especially financial supported. Political leaders who have never served in the military forces become decision makers of war. This is a backward decision that this country has failed to consider when voting. Veterans are injured mentally and physically and left to continue our lives with limited resources and under extreme conditions. After military services discharge, we are left fighting for our well-deserved benefits. Service members are discriminated and treated unfairly in the job force too. Veterans have service experience working for the government, and yet we are judged unfairly for the federal positions. The government jobs description states veterans' preference, but the additional requirement or stipulations eliminate veterans' preference. Why do the people who have served this country become dirt to our government system? Most veterans has become alien from the states after serving. There is no such thing as free medical care when all health concerns are limited to coverage. Veterans should be on the priority list of citizens along with the teachers, police officers, children, pastors, fire fighters, and God. Pastors help put people's lives back on track when our government steps on it. I say, pay the pastors congress salary.

First Lady Obama is fighting for good health in the food that we eat. She has been campaigning for healthy diets worldwide. Some countries are not in a financial or agricultural position to grow or practice healthy eating. However, United States seems to have the resources to get on board. If we look at obesity in our families alone, there is an urgent need to start practicing a longer healthy living. Everywhere you go, there are people seen struggling to walk or having difficulty with breathing. Our children are not able to meet most standard exercise requirements needed to keep their bodies healthy.

Obesity is affecting our relationships with our spouses and other people. Yet the media have allowed advertisements on any and everything unhealthy that can contribute to our death. If you look healthy, you get accused of starving or having surgery to prevent obesity. It is inconvenient to others and dangerous to some to be overweight. It can prevent you from flying or driving. It is impossible to sit beside an obese person or become intimately involved with one. Sometimes our children are victimized by others because of their weight. Granted that there are all sizes and shapes of people, but let us be healthy with our figure. If your weight is causing a health problem, then we may need to get in check and practice healthy living.

Is it necessary to have banks manage money? Is it necessary to pay taxes to the government? One fines you for what you have, and one penalizes you for what you do not have. However, they both record and maintain your life. Neither one of them have your best interest. Credit is no longer a straight look into one's eyes with a firm right handshake. It is bad as a citizen to need credit, but your poor credit rating limits you from borrowing. Yet our government gives billions of money to other countries that are not rated by our credit system that we the citizens are rated. Other countries never pay us back, and we do not hold their creditability when they ask for additional money. This is how our government treats citizens. It is better to be a noncitizen; it comes with great benefits. Immigrants and noncitizens receive credit assistance to help establish their lives and choose their lifestyles. When a person dies, in the majority cases, their wealth is not buried along with them. So, why is this country denying all citizens from having a rich and fulfilled style of living?

Technology has taken off like a rocket lost in space. It has advance so far ahead of man we are trailing behind it. This is why we need to invest in our teachers and youth of the future. To gain knowledge, we must make change. President Obama relates to technology well because he interacts with the people of the United States through his work. The Internet is working in favor of those who understand the needs of people and are able to communicate effectively for the good of mankind.

Word of mouth is a network base itself. The purpose of Facebook and Twitter should be used wisely to spread good communication globally. If you do not have anything good to share with the world, then stay off the net! America is going nowhere, fast. The nerve of the anti-citizens to go public, blathering our president's administration. To be honest, calculation does not put Obama in thought of being born at the beginning of this country's debt.

Have you driven a vehicle on the roads and highways in this country? Why is the government struggling to invest in this country traveling/transportation system? Are we that concerned about restructuring of other countries that we are willing to sacrifice the safety of our citizens? We are willing to neglect our land to help rebuild other country's roads, what a shame. Our metro system is below advance technology compared to other countries, which we give trillions to help rebuild and restore their economy. This country needs to vote on reformation of Obama's term to allow him to assist with reformation of the United States system and reestablish the citizens' lives. Self-employed opportunities is hard to obtain but a given for immigrants and noncitizens. Most people no longer own a home to establish an independent business. When our uncaring government joined in with the mortgage industry and foreclosed properties, most businesses was seized too. Ask the Internal Revenue Services, they played a role in this devastating economy. Rising property taxes to make a buck. This independent action caused homeowners to pay for their property twice! It is bad enough that the safety of this country is a high risk.

So how safe is the food we consume daily. Does anyone cook from home, or even know how to operate a cooking range? At a buffet, people dig and scratch their skin and handle the serving ware to get their food. Some have colds and open wounds or scaling, and they reach over the food items. Children are not being watched, and they handle food items like Play-doh. Visit most fast foods restaurants and go into their bathroom, and you will quickly become familiar with your oven range. Some stores are not properly informing their customers on food condition or expiration of use. The FDA (Food and Drug Administration) are just like the system—they work against the people. There is food imported into United States from countries with poor health and placed on the shelves within the food industry.

Gas prices are up, and the only people not complaining are the policy makers within our government system. Racism, prejudice, discrimination are still in existence. Some are no longer color driven but power structured. It has shifted to same race group, siblings on siblings, relatives against in-laws, churches against government, and on one's self. However, we can participate in becoming better people and eliminate these injustice in our country. It is written on the good book to treat one another with love. How can we the people continue to sit back and watch destruction of another human. This is a prime example of adult bullying.

Bullying carries heavy trait of manipulation and destruction of a person character. All of mankind is from the same blood tribe of Abraham. We may not all sleep together but must get along for the sake of America's future. The example that we show on how we mistreat our president is what triggers how the other countries view us. When we degrade our president, and then other countries follow the degrading. Utilizing the media to talk negative about our president makes one look foolish and unethical to believe or trust. If you were the president, would you want your citizens bad mouthing you? What a shame and sadness that one spends so much time tearing down another human being. Treat others the right and respectful way! The

United States is a pride-driven base of worldly people. Pride that makes us look over the citizens' weakness and will to help others.

Charity begins at home land first! A reputation of fine wine with beer assets. The leaders in this country are tearing down the strength of each others and destroying our world peace. Just think of how great and powerful we could present America if we stood on the United Nation under one God! My opinion is that the United States is in need of reformation. We need to get rid of our old established ways. We need to release the embedded founders of this expired government system. Let us put away in history the way of running this country and change with the time. People do not even think or feel the way the past operated. This is why there is an Old and New Testament day! It is time America learns from the past and transform into the future. The embedded ones have marked history and will forever be remembered, but we must move forward. This country is being held in bondage with the past worldly leaders, and they have far gone. This is why our young people are detaching themselves away from the government system. They have come to the conclusion that it does not work for their parents or them! We can not continue to build for the past, and the people have changed into the future. Technology is a prime example why we must change our government system and the leaders within it. My opinion as a United States citizen is that we must reform if there is to be a future in America.

www.ingramcontent.com/pod-product-compliance
Ingram Content Group UK Ltd.
Pitfield, Milton Keynes, MK11 3LW, UK
UKHW022217230426
12048UKWH00016BA/905